Benn Pitman, Andrew Jackson Graham

Exhibit of the State of the Phonographic Art

Benn Pitman, Andrew Jackson Graham

Exhibit of the State of the Phonographic Art

ISBN/EAN: 9783337407636

Printed in Europe, USA, Canada, Australia, Japan

Cover: Foto ©Thomas Meinert / pixelio.de

More available books at **www.hansebooks.com**

EXHIBIT

OF THE

STATE OF THE PHONOGRAPHIC ART,

WITH REFERENCE TO THE COPYRIGHT CASE

OF

GRAHAM *vs.* PITMAN,

IN THE UNITED STATES CIRCUIT COURT FOR THE SOUTHERN DISTRICT OF OHIO, IN EQUITY.

By ANDREW J. GRAHAM.

New York:
ANDREW J. GRAHAM,
491 BROADWAY.

PREFACE.

§ 1. Part I. of this exhibit is an alphabetical list of the words, to which, and their forms, positions, and other features and facts, attention is to be directed. The order of investigation should be this:

I. Let the word be observed.

II. Note the forms, positions, etc., presented at the left. When a form is given without any authority, it is given as the form inferred from the knowledge of the general state of the art, as presented by Isaac Pitman, preceding the Hand-Book, excepting his then unsettled tenth edition. Variances from such general state are shown by references to the author presenting them. I. P. 9th, or 9 ed., or Voc., are references to the general state of Phonography immediatly preceding the Hand-Book. I. P. '46, or I. P. Rep., refers to an early preceding state of the art, many of whose forms, positions, etc., had been abandoned, as will appear by reference to later editions. And it should be noted, that the word "edition" has been used by I Pitman and generally by Phonographers, as in this exhibit, to denote different modifications, forms, or states of Phonography. Generally, if the Hand-Book forms (shown at the right of the word) should appear to be old, then attention is called to a new position or disposal of the word, to distinguish it from other words. Sometimes a new positional arrangement of word-forms allows the safe use of an old form which had been abandoned. If the Hand-Book position should be old, then attention is generally directed to a new form. If the Hand-Book forms and positions should appear to have been in use *immediately preceding the Hand-Book,* as shown by the references, then, the word is introduced for comparison simply with other words, generally indented, that is, placed a little to the right of the general left-hand line of the column.

III. Observe the Hand-Book outlines, whether new in general *form,* by *contraction* of old form, or by using *one* form for two, three, four, or more words, for which *more* or *different* forms were used in the Old Phonography.

IV. Observe the forms in the last column, devoted to the Reporter's Companion of the defendant. If the Companion form is the same, *in every respect,* as the Hand-Book form preceding, that fact is shown by the contraction *do.* for *ditto.* If the Companion form is, in any respect, different from the Hand-Book form, that difference is indicated, and attention is otherwise called to the likeness, as likeness in form (which will appear by a mere comparison); likeness in representing a similar portion of the word, less than the whole; likeness in representing different words by one form, differently represented in the Old Phonography.

If the Companion form should have no resemblance to the Hand-Book form, or its position, etc., then attention is directed simply to the word, as a part of a reporter's list.

§ 2. The phrase "in no old R. L." (Reporting List) has reference to the Reporting Lists of Isaac Pitman, Paterson, Parkhurst, Graham, and Benn Pitman, *preceding the Hand-Book.*

§ 3. References to pages, sections, etc., are to the book near whose name, or in whose column, they are placed. References to the Hand-Book, unless otherwise specified, are to Part II.

§ 4. References to I. P. 10—Isaac Pitman's Tenth Edition, are, when occuring be fore the word, to lists of reporting word-signs, published before the Hand-Book when occurring to the right of the word, the references are to a publication after the Hand-Book.

§ 5. Quotations of words, as "Instruction, in (the) construction," are intended to show the precise arrangement of words in the book to which the column is appropriated.

§ 6. The portion of a word represented by a contraction is frequently written after or below the contraction.

§ 7. Words are, in a few cases, introduced, when no claim is made in respect to them, to show a secured harmony or consistency of writing a derivitive or related word—as *Character,* to show the harmony of the Hand-Book forms for *Character* and *Characteristic;* remedying the confusing unlikeness of forms in the Old Phonography, namely, *Character,* Ker^2-Kay; Est^1-Kay, *Characteristic.*

§ 8. CONTRACTIONS.

A. & B.—Andrews and Boyles' First Reporter's Book, 1850.
acs.—advanced corresponding style.
B. P.—Benn Pitman.
B. P. V.—Benn Pitman's Vocabulary, published in 1854, after R. M. [Graham's Reporter's Manual], and before the Hand-Book.
cs.—corresponding style.
do.—*ditto*, the same as at the left; ["]—the same as above.
Gra.—Graham.
H. B.—Hand-Book.
I. P.—Isaac Pitman.
I. P. '46.—Isaac Pitman's Reporter, 1846.
l.—list, as 1st l., first list.
p.—position, as 1 p., first position, i. e., *above* the line; 2 p., second position, i. e. *on* the line; 3 p., third position, i. e., *through* or *below* the line.
Park.—Parkhurst.
Pat.—Paterson.
phr.—phrase-writing.
Phr. B.—Phrase-Book, new edition, 1862, after H. B.
R. C.—Benn Pitman's Reporter's Companion—after the Hand-Book.
R. L.—Reporting List.
R. M.—Reporter's Manual, by Graham.
rs.—reporting style.
Sk.—Biographical Sketch. 1856.
Voc.—Vocabulary, by Isaac Pitman, according to the 9th edition of Phonography.
ws.—word-sign; *dws.*—derivitive word-sign, i. e., a sign derived from another word by the rules of the Hand-Book.
1 p.—first position, i. e., *above* the line.
2 p.—second position, i. e., *on* the line.
3 p.—third position, i. e., *through* or *below* the line.
9 C.—Ninth edition Reporter's Companion, by Isaac Pitman, 1852-3.
10 C.—Tenth edition " " "
9 ed.—Ninth edition.
10 ed.—Tenth edition.

§ 9. Dates are contracted thus, '46, '47.

§ 10 DATES OF DIFFERENT PHONOGRAPHIC PUBLICATIONS.

Isaac Pitman's REPORTER 1846
Parkhurst's MAGAZINES .... 1849—1853
Paterson 1850
Isaac Pitman's 9 ed REPORTER'S COMPANION 1854
Graham's REPORTER'S MANUAL—R. M. .... early in 1854
Benn Pitman's VOCABULARY—B. P. or B. P. V. .... later in 1854
SKETCH of Dr. James W. Stone, ... 1856
"I. P. 10," at the left of the words, refers to lists published in 1857
HAND-BOOK .... October, 1858
Benn Pitman's PHRASES, old edition 1859
new edition 1862
Benn Pitman's REPORTER'S COMPANION. Its first list, corresponding to Hand-Book List of Reporting Word-signs, was published in his Magazine, in Aug., 1860
The entire book was published in 1861

§ 11. The facts of this exhibit are presented for the just consideration of all concerned. No one's judgment could be aided by mere declamation.

Exhibit.

PART I.

Preceding the Hand-Book.	Hand-Book		Rep. Comp.
. (heavy dot), Sk. or joined	A	or joined §71	do
. (light dot), "	An		
. (light dot); R.M. §90, - horizontal tick) joined; Sk. - or joined	And		
Not in B.P.V.	Able to have		do
	Abrupt		do
	Abruptness		
B.P.V. do	Accuracy		
B.P.V. do	Accurate		do.
	Acquainted	acquaint'...	...do
	Acquainted		
	Acquaintance		
Not in B.P.V.	Active	activ'.....	...do
	Activity		

Admit
Admitted } admit — do
Admittance
2d p and En-stroke — Admonish
" " — Admonished } 3d p and En-hook
" " — Admonition
1st p and En-stroke — Diminish
" " — Diminished } 2d p and En-hook
" " — Diminution
Dominate-d-ant }
2d p — Domination } 1st p.
2d p. & Con-dot. BPV. 1st p — Condemnation 2d p — do
Damnation — do
Not in BPV. — Advance } — do
" — Advanced }
" — Advancement — do
IP 10. — Divine } — do
Dimity }
Differ
Differed } — do
3d p — Different
3d p — Difference
Difficult-y — do

Park	Advertise			
"	Advertised			do
"	Advertisement			
Not in B.P.V	Dollar			do
; BPV	Defendant			do
Not in B.P.V	Aggrandise			
"	Aggrandizement			
"	Aggregate			
"	Aggregated	aggregā'		do
"	Aggregation			
"	Allegory			
"	Allegorical	allegor'		do
; cautioned against in TP Rep. 246, and then given in phr. only	Almighty			do
	Almightiness	almight'		wanting
	Ambiguity	ambig'		do. 3d p
; BPV	Amelioration		See under Melioration	do
; BPV	Melioration			do
	Anchor			
	Anchored	§207, R 4; §168, R 8		do

Notes	Word	Pronunciation / remarks	
; Not in B.P.V	Angel	a'jel	do
"	Archangel	ar'jel	do
	Evangel	a'jel — Not given but "Evangelic," &c	
Not in B.P.V	Angelic	'jelic	do
P. Park 2^d p. ; gl, BPV 2^d N	Evangelic-al	'ajel'	do
in full. Not in BPV nor any other old R.L.	Anglo-Saxon	contracted	do
; ged " = n wm	Animal	large El-hook p. 80. R. 2	do
Not in BPV nor any other old R.L.	Animal Kingdom, acs, rs		do
Not in B.P.V	Another one		do
	Any other one		wanting
; ; BP do	In their own, dws,	p. 211, R. 1	do
ged. Not in BPV nor any other old R.L.	No other one		do
Not in B.P.V	Antagonist }		
"	Antagonistic }		
"	Antagonism		do. 2^d p
; rarely in phr; used to be Perfect	Appear		do
	Appeared		do
; BPV do	Appearance		do
; Ar B '50 Not in BPV	Appliance		do
; " "	Compliance		do

		Approach } Approachable }		do
Not in B.P.V.				
"	I.P.10	Approve }		do
"	wanting	Approval }		
		Prove		do
		Proof		do
	Not in I.P.10	Perfect		do
	I.P.10	Approved		do
Not in I.P.10.	Not in B.P.V	Profit-ed-able }		do
"	"	Prophet }		
I.P.10		Proved		do
Not in B.P.V		Approximate }		
"		Approximated }		do 3p
"		Approximation }	approx[n]	do
"		Archangel		do
Not in B.P.V		Arithmetic }		
"		Arithmetical }		do
"		Arithmetician }	arithmet[n]	

Outline	Note	Word	Contracted	
[shorthand]		Arrange	[shorthand] arrange'	[shorthand]
[shorthand]	[shorthand] B.P.V	Arrangement		do
[shorthand]		Artificial	[shorthand] contracted	[shorthand]
[shorthand] in full	Not in B.P.V.	Artificiality		[shorthand] do
[shorthand]	Not in B.P.V	As it had	[shorthand]	do
[shorthand]	"	As it ought	[shorthand]	not given
[shorthand]	B.P.V [shorthand]	As it would	[shorthand]	do
[shorthand]	Not in B.P.V.	As it had not, dws,	[shorthand]	do
[shorthand]	B.P.V [shorthand]	As it would	[shorthand]	do.
[shorthand]		As it would have, dws,	[shorthand]	do
[shorthand]		As it would have had, dws,	[shorthand]	do
[shorthand]		As it would not, dws,	[shorthand]	do
[shorthand]		Ascend	[shorthand] ascend'	
[shorthand]	Not in B.P.V	Ascended		do
[shorthand]	"	Ascendancy		
[shorthand]	"	Ascribe	[shorthand] p.193, R.1; p.168, R.8	
[shorthand]	"	Ascribed		do
[shorthand]	[shorthand] Art 3, R.M. p.117 [shorthand] Not in B.P.V.	Assignment	[shorthand]	do

; Park	Astronomy		in full
in full Not in B.P.V	Astronomical	contracted	do
	Astronomer		wanting
Not in BPV	At first		do
	At it		do
At B '50 ; ged. Not in BPV "ought to, it ought to"	It ought		do
	It had		do
Park. 2d p. ged. B.P.V do	It would		do
; Not in B.P.V	At length		do
"	At one		do
2d p & Con-dot BPV Contains	Contain	distinguished by position	do
2d p. Never made a w.s.	Attain		
Not in B.P.V nor any other old R.L	Atlantic Ocean		do
"	Atmosphere		
"	Atmospheric		
"	Atmospherical	at'spher'	atmosphe'
BPV	Attainable		do 2d p
Not in BPV nor any other old R.L.	Attraction of Gravitation	contracted	

Outline	Remarks	Word		
	In no old R.L.	Augment		
	"	Augmented		do 1st p
	"	Augmentation	augment'	
	"	Auspicious		
	"	Auspiciously		do
	"	Auspiciousness		
Voc;	Park. Not in B.P.V	Authentic		
"	In no old R.L.	Authenticity	or	authentist'- do
	Not in B.P.V	Authoritative		
	"	Authority	authorit'	do
	Not in B.P.V nor any other old R.L.	Average	av'age	do
; A+B.	Park. Not in BPV	Averse		do
; BPV do		Universe		do
; Park '49		Converse		not given but "Conversion"
2d p	Not in B.P.V	Aversion		do
"	"	Conversion		do
"	"	Version		do
IP. 46;	Voc. Not in B.P.V	Averte		do
" ;	" "	Averted		
" ;	BPV IP10 do	Virtue		do

; Not in B.P.V. nor any other old R. L.	Overwork		do in 1st L.
Voc. "	Conceit-ed		do in 2nd L.
; B.P.V. do	Awful		
Not in B.P.V.	Awfulness	awf'	awful'

B

	Bankable	ba. g b	do
— Not in B.P.V. nor any other old R. L.	Bank		
; G. ; 2nd p. ; B.P.V. do	Bankrupt	bang'	do
; " "	Bankruptcy		
Not in B.P.V. nor any other old R. L.	Beginner		do
"	Begun		do
"	Began	gan / gun	do
in phr. only. In no old list of word-signs	Behind	"Combined, Behind"	"Behind, Combined"
	Be-not		do
Not in B.P.V.	Benefactor		
Not in B.P.V. nor any other old R. L.	Beneficent	contracted	do
"	Beneficence	benef'	do
"	Beneficial		
	Bespeak	contracted	do

Remarks	Word		
Not in B.P.V nor any other old R.L	Bigot		
"	Bigoted		do
"	Bigotry		
"	Biography		
"	Biographic		
"	Biographical		
"	Bounty		
"	Bountiful	but	but
rarely in phr. Not in B.P.V	Brethren See Brother		do
Not in B.P.V nor in any other old R.L	Brokenhearted	brokenheart	do
rarely in phr. Not in B.P.V	Brother		do
Not in B.P.V	Brotherly, &c.,		do
Voc. Not in B.P.V nor any other old R.L	Burdensome		do
Not in P's Voc "	Busybody		

C.

Remarks	Word		
In no old R.L Not in B.P.V	Calculable		Contracted
Not in B.P.V	Calculate-d		
"	Calculation		
; B.P.V do	California		
Not in B.P.V nor any other old R.L	Call forth		do

Authority	Word	Form	
Not in B.P.V	Carefully		do
Not in B.P.V nor any other old R.L	Category		
"	Categorical	categor	do
SP 46; 9 C; 10 C, and B.P.V	Catholic		
Not in B.P.V nor any other old R.L	Catholicism		do See Roman Catholicism
BPV	Challenge		
wanting	Challenged	chalej	do
Not in B.P.V nor any other old R.L	Challenger	chalejer	do
Not in BPV nor any other old R.L.	Change		
"	Changed	chā	chāj
"	Changeable-y	contracted	do
9 C & BPV	Character		do
9 C, BPV; Pat; Park	Characteristic		do
BPV	Charge		
	Charged		
Not in BPV nor any other old R.L	Chargeable	H.B. [illegible]	

Not in B.P.V	Charitable		
(… on charity) Not in B.P.V	Charity	Cha	do
…	Cheered	Chd	do
Park	Cheerful-ly		
…	Cheerfulness	3 words by one sign	
…	Cheer		do
… Chair, wh. are	Chair, Which are		do
Not in B.P.V nor any other old R.L.	Which were		do
"	Which are to have		do
"	Which are of		do
"	Which were to have		do
"	Which were of		do
Not in B.P.V	Chemical-ly		do
"	Chemistry	Chem	do
Park "	Christianize		
		ize by a circle	do
rs 2d p always BPV	Circumstance		
RM 2d p. Not in BPV	Circumstantial		do
Not in B.P.V nor any other old R.L.	Collateral	Collat	do
BPV	Collect		
RM do; BPV	Collected	1st p.	do

Not in B.P.V	Collective	unidbe		Unchanged H.B. Christian and Production
2d p. R.M. 54 "	Combination			do
2d p. Never made a no "	Common			do
B.P.V do	Country			do
Not in B.P.V	Commonest			do
"	Commonly			do
A & B Not in B.P.V	Compliance			do
Not in B.P.V nor any other old R.L	Comprehensible			
" B.P.V gives Comprehend and	Comprehensibility			
" Apprehend	Apprehensible-bility			H.B. sign for -ble -bility and distinguishing by position as H.B does
SP10 Not in B.P.V Conclude	Conclude-d	p. 168. R.8		do
Not in B.P.V nor any other old R.L	Conformable-y	i.e. Conformb'		do
Not in B.P.V nor any other old R.L	Conjecture			
"	Conjectured	'jek'		'jekt' apparently, but see Misconjecture
"	Conjectural			
"	Misconjecture	mis'jek'		do

; Fack. Not in BPV nor in any other old R.L.	Conscientious		
wanting "	Conscientiously		
"	Conscientiousness	p193, R.L.	
IP46; BPV do.	Consequential		do in 1st l.
	Consider		
BPV	Considerable-y	consider	do
IP44; IP46 BP'34 IP10	Consist		do
IP44; IP46 BP'34 IP10	System	syst	do
IP46; ged Not in BPV	Consisted		do
"; ged + BPV + IP10 do.	Consistence		do
Not in BPV	Sustains, -ers,		do
; BPV	Consistency	1st l.	do
Not in BPV.	Sustain		do
BPV	Consistent		do
Not in BPV	Sustained		do
Not in BPV nor any other old R.L.	Conspicuous		
"	Conspicuously		
"	Conspicuousness	3 words, one form	
IP46; Pink. Voc. RM Not in BPV p118	Consentment		do

		Word		
IP 46 B.P 54	RM p 7	Constitute		do
IP 46;	Voc and BPV; RM p 118	Constituted		
"	" " " RM	Stated		do
Voc. Not in B.P.V nor any other old R.L		Constitutionality		
2d p. never made a ws		Contain	st. tshn. t... Both distinguish by position	do
2d p. In no old list of word-signs. Not in B.P.V		Attain		
Never in any old list of word-signs. Not in B.P.V		At one		do
2d p B.PV 2d p		Contains	Both distinguish by position	do
2d p Not in B.P.V		Attains		
2d p Not in B.P.V		Contract	Both give one form for the present and past tense, and distinguish by position; viz, the 2d and 3d	
"	"	Contracted		
"	"	Attract		
"	"	Attracted		
	"	Contradictory	contradict'	do
Not a word-sign in LP 10. Not in B.P.V		Contrive-ance		
"		Contrived		do
2d p Not made a ws. Not in B.P.V		Conversion		do
" Not made a ws		Version		do
" Not in B.P.V	"	Aversion		do

2d p. Not in B.P.V nor any other old R.L	Convert		do
	Converted		
" "	Over it		Do
I.P. 46 I.P. 10 B.P.V	Virtue		do
averted I.P. 46 ged Not in B.P.V	Avert-ed		do
B.P.V	Correct		
"	Corrected		
Not in B.P.V	Correctness	out of strict position	
I.P. 10	Corrective	In both books, Correct + ive out of strict p.	
	Careful		do
B.P.V do	Correspond		
Not in B.P.V	Corresponded	p. 193. R. 3	do
Park	Correspondence		
B.P.V B.P.V	Country		do
Not in B.P.V	Common		do
"	Countryman		
"	Countrymen		
In no [illegible] list of word signs but N. & B. 1 v. Not in B.P.V	Creation	sh p	do
Not in B.P.V nor any other old R.L.	Creative		

In no old list of contns	Crim*in*ate			
" " " " "	Criminated			
; in R. M p111 Criminal jurisprudence	Criminal			
In no old R. L	Cross-examination			
in full "	Cross-examine	i.e. omitting K of ex and S of Cross		do
in full "	Cross-examined			do
In no old R. L except R. M p118	Culpable			
In no old R. L	Culpability			
	Cultivate-d	p 193, R1		do
B.P.	Cure		Ker[3]	do
Never contracted B.P. ,	Correct-ed		Ker[1]	
In no old list of word-signs B.P.	Accuracy		Ker[3]	
,	Cured		Kret[3]	do
B.P. " " " " " "	Accurate		Kret[3]	do
" " " " " "	Cures			do
; B.P. " " " " " "	Curious			do

D.

Never made a word-sign in full & Not in B.P.V.	Dark	Der[3]	do
" " " " "	Darken	Dren[3]	do
" " " " "	Darkened		

	Never made a word-sign and not in B.P.V.	Darkens	Drens[3] in 1st b	do
	" " "	Darkness	" "	do
	In no old R. L. Not in BPV.	Decapitate		
	" " " "	Decapitated		do
	" " " "	Decapitation	i.e. decapit'	
	In no old R. L.	Declaim	Declaim	
	First contracted in	Declamation	Declamatory	
	the H. B.	Declamatory	Declamation	
		Exclaim-ed-ation	contracted	do
	S.P. '46 B.L. '54	Declare		
	" B.L. '54	Declared	i.e. dklr	i.e. dklr
	" ; Park Not in B.P.V. First one sign in H.B.	Declaration		
	B.P.	Defendant	Dee[2]	do
	Not in BPV.	Dollar	Dee[1]	do
	Park only; B.L. '54	Advertised-ment	Dee[3]	do
	First contracted in	Deform		
	Not given B.P. the Hand Book list, and in no	Deformed	Dee[4]	do
	old list for Reporters, but Graham's, 1854	Deformity	defor'	
	In no old R. L.	Degradation	degrad'	do

In no old R. L. and	Deject			
first provided with a	Dejected			
contraction in the Hand Book	Dejection	dj		i.e. djkt tho' there is no t in dejection
In no old R. L. Voc	Delicacy			
		del- represented by an El-hook sign		
Voc In no old R. L.	Delicate			do
" " " " "	Delicateness			
J.P. 46 B.P. 52	Delight			do
"	Delighted			
	Delinquent &c only place on p. 26			
In no old R. L.	Depart			do
" " " "	Departed	depart'		
" " " "	Department			
	Defend			do
	Depended			
; (depen') Park & B.P.	Dependence			do
; " " "	Dependent			do
In no old R. L.	Depravity	i.e. deprav'		do 2d p.
In no old R. L. and	Deprecate			
first contracted in H.B.	Deprecated			
	Deprecation	i.e. depr'		i.e. deprecat' altho' no t sound occurs in Deprecation

Voc. In no old R.L — Derange } do
" " — Derangement }

Voc In no old R.L — Deride } Drd' do
" " — Derided }

SP46 First one sign in H.T.B. — Dread } Dred² do
Dreaded }

In no old R.L. — Duringit — Dred³ do

SP46; Pat. do. Never made a w.s. not in B.P 54 — Derision — Dershon' do

Ged. In no old R.L — Direction — Dershon² not given

SP46; Pat. do. R.M p.36. B.P after R.M — Duration — Dershon³ do

Voc — Derivation. cs. (p.169 Read Ex; rs) do

" In no old R.L. — Derivative

Voc. Never made a w.s. — Derive — Dref' do

Derived — Dreft' do

In no old R.L — Derogation

" " " " — Derogatory — contracted do

SP46; Park; Ged 10ed B.P — Describe } do
" " " " — Described }

" B.P " probably — Description do

In no old R.L	Descriptive Descriptiveness		do
SP46 tho' Observe is & / & Park. Not in 9th ed and not in B.P	Deserve Deserved	&	do
SP46 In no late R.L / not in B.P.V.	Desirable	desir'	do
In no old Reporting List, and first contracted in the Hand Book	Despicable Despicableness	i.e. despic'	do
In no old R.L " " " "	Despot Despotic	i.e. despot'	do
Voc. In no late R.L	Despotism		do
SP46; 9 Ed; R.M. B.P.V.	Destruction		do
In no old R.L	Destructive		do.
SP46 In no later R.L	Determination	deter'ashon	do
SP46. In no other R.L B.P Voc. In, no old R.L.	Determine Determinable	deter'n'	do
B.P. Voc. In no old R.L.	Determined Determinedly	deter'nd'	do
In no old R.L	Detest-ation	in H.15	In R.C
B.P. , Not in B.P. Voc	Detriment Detrimental	aes; rs p.118. R5;	

In no old R. L.	Devote	In H. B. contracted		In R. L. contracted
Voc In no old R. L. but B. P.	Dexterity	in accordance with p. 111. R. 4		do.
In no old R. L.	Diameter	}		do.
" " " "	Diametrical	}		
Not in B. P. V. 10 ed	Differ	}		
" "	Differed	} Def[2]		do.
P. 46 B. P. "	Different	}		
" "	Difference	}		
difficult " y P. 46 9 ed 10 ed	Difficult-y			do
; rs ; 10 ed divine, and adver-tise-is-ment	Divine	} Def'		do
; Not in B. P. V. 10 ed	Divinity	}		
Not in B. P. V.	Advance-d	Def[3]		do
In no old R. L. Not in B. P. V.	Dignify	}		
" " " "	Dignified	} dig'		do.
9 ed & B. P.	Dignity	}		
P. 46 ; Voc Not in B. P. V.	Delinquent	} Del for del- and contracted		
" " " "	Delinquency	}		do
Voc In no old R. L.	Dilapidate	}		
" "	Dilapidated	} dilapid'		do
" "	Dilapidation	}		

Shorthand	Note	Word	Remarks
[shorthand]	1st p and Ew stroke B.P. 34	Diminish	[shorthand] [shorthand] [shorthand] [shorthand] 2d p. + Ew hook .... do
[shorthand]	"	Diminished	
[shorthand]	"	Diminution	
		See Admonish &c	
[shorthand]	In no old R. L	Diplomat	[shorthand] i.e. diplomat' do
[shorthand]	"	Diplomatic	
[shorthand]	S.P. 46; B.P. do	Direct	[shorthand] Dir2 [shorthand] one form for both present and past tense.
[shorthand]	In no old R. L	Directed	
[shorthand]	Voc In no old R. L	Directory	[shorthand] contracted [shorthand] contd
[shorthand]	" "	Director	[shorthand] " do
[shorthand]	In no old Reporting list, and first provided with one form in the H.B.	Disappoint	[shorthand] do. 3/p. 1st p. necy to accented vowel
[shorthand]		Disappointed	
[shorthand]		Disappointment	
[shorthand]	In no old R. L	Discountenance	[shorthand] [shorthand] present and past tense alike
[shorthand]	"	Discountenanced	
	In no old R. L	Discordant	In H.B. In R. C.
[shorthand]; [shorthand]	in ed. In no old R.L	Discover	[shorthand] i.e. discov' do
[shorthand]; [shorthand]	" "	Discovered	
[shorthand]; [shorthand]	" "	Discovery	
[shorthand] [shorthand]	In no old R. L	Discrepancy	[shorthand] [illegible] ancy [shorthand] [illegible]

In no old R.L.	Discriminate			
"	Discriminated			
Park Not in B.P.U.	Discrimination	contracted	do	
In no old R.L.	Dishonor			
"	Dishonorable		do	
In no old R.L.	Disparage			
"	Disparagement		do	
In no old R.L.	Disqualify			
"	Disqualification			
In no old R.L.	Dissatisfy			
	Dissatisfied	Dissatisfy " ied		
	Dissatisfaction			
In no old R.L.	Distinctive			
In no old R.L.	Distinguishable		do	
; 1P10 ... Def[1]	Divine	Bee for -ble Def[1]	do	
" Not in B.P.U.	Divinity			
; ired ... Def[3]	Differ-ed-ent-ence	Def[2]	do	
; ; 1P10 Def[2]	Difficult-y		do	
; not in 10 ed. Not in B.P.U.	Advance-d	Def[3]	do	

In no old R. L.	Divine Being		
"	Divulge in H.B.		In R.C.
SP'46 Park do	Doctrine		
B.P. Voc wanting In no old R. L	Doctrinal		do
Never contracted Not in B.P.T.	Darken-ed		do
In no old R. L	Dollar	Dee	do
BP '54	Defendant	Dee2	do
Park only	Adjective-d-ment	Dee3	do
Was 2d p.	Domination 1st p. in 413		do in R.C.
B.P.T.	Doubt-ed, wd be		do
In no old R. L	Downcast	n omitted	do
Voc "	Downfall	"	do
" "	Downhearted	downheart'	do
SP'46	Downright	dow'right	do
In no old R. L. Not in Voc.	Downtrod-den	dow'trod'	do
SP'46; in full	Downward		
R.M. [subsequently BPT]	Duration.	n omitted See Derision	do do
Never made a word-sign	During it		do
Not in B.P.T. In no old R. L.	Dwellinghouse	dwell' house	do
"	Dwellingplace	dwell' place	do

Voc. In no old R. L.	Dyspepsia		
" "	Dyspeptic		do

E.

In no old R. L.	Each will		do
"	Much will		do
"	Eastern		do
"	Eccentric		
"	Eccentricity	eccentri'	do
9th ed.	Ecclesiastic		do
9 ed	Ecclesiastical		not given
Voc. IP46	Economy		do
Not given in Voc. Not in IPH	Economical		
In no old R. L	Efficaciously	In H. B	In R C
In no old R. L	Efficient		do
"	Efficiency	efish'	
In no old R. L.	Electro		not given
	Electric		do
	Electricity		
Voc In no old R. L	Emphatic		do
Not in Voc. In no old R. L	Emphatical		

Voc In no old R.L.[2]	Endanger			do
1 IP46 In no other old R.L	Enlarge	}		do
B.P. Not in Rep. 46 In no old R.L. Not in B.P.V.	Enlargement	}		
In no old R.L but Graham's 54 p. 119	Entangle	}		
In no old R.L	Entangled	}		
"	Entanglement	one form for three words.		
; B.P. do "	Enthusiast	}	Enthusias	}
In no old R.L	Enthusiastic	}	Enthusiastical	}
; B.P. do	Enthusiasm	enthusias' i.e. contracted.		Contracted
IP46 ed Not in B.P.V.	Entire		Enter'	do
	In their		Endher'	do
	Another	p. 211	Enther[2]	do
Not in B.P.V.	No other		Endher[3]	do
IP46; ed B.P.	Entirely			do
Voc In no old R.L	Envelop			not given
" "	Enveloped or be			do
In no old R.L.	Episcopal	}		
"	Episcopalian	}		do
"	Episcopacy	}		

Sources / remarks		Word	Form	
I P'46; small hook	ged " B.P.	Eternal	etern'.	do
2P'46;	" in full; B.P. do.	Eternity		
I P'46	Gra. '54 B.P.	Eternal life		do
Not in B.P.T "		Evangelic	gel'	
(Jel'2) Park;	ged " B.P. 2dp	Evangelical		do
I P'46 + B.P. '54		Evangelisation, drvs.		do
	B.P.	Evangelise		do
	2dp B.P.	Evangelised, drvs.		do
I P10	2dp Not in B.P.T	Evening		do
I P'46;	46; R.M. B.P. "	Everyone		do
Voc	In no old R.L	Exceptionable	Bee for ble	do
In no old R.L		Exclaim		
		Exclaimed		do
		Exclamation		
		Exclamatory		
In no old R.L		Exclude		
"		Excluded	or	
In no old R.L		Exemplify	Both using present for the past tense.	
"		Exemplified		
"		Exemplification	i.e. 'semp' i.e. egsamp'	

	Note	Word		
	In no old R.L	Exhibit		
	"	Exhibited	zibit'	ygzibit'
	In no old R.L	Exhibition	In the H.P.	In R.C
	In no old R.L and Existed not in Voc	Exist-ed-ence	In the H.P.	In R.C.
	Voc. In no old R.L	Expansibility		
	I.P.'46 Not in B.P.'41	Experience	'sperience	do
	" "	Experienced	'sperienced	do
	I.P.'46; B.P. do	Explain		
	" "	Explanation	i.e. 'splain'	i.e. explain'
wanting	Voc. In no old R.L	Explanatory		
	In no old R.L	Exterminate		
	"	Exterminated	'stermin'	ekstermin
	"	Extermination		
	I.P.'46; B.P. do	Extravagant		
	; (large loop) Park Not in B.P.'41	Extreme		
	In no old R.L	Extremity	contracted	Contracted

F.

		Word		
Voc	In no old R.L	Facetious		do
		Facetiously		
"		Facetiousness		
	In no old R.L	Factious		
		Factiously		
		Factiousness	p. 193. R.3	
		Factitious-ly-ness wd be p193, R.3		do
	In no old R.L	Fainthearted-ness	In H.B & Contd	In R.C and Contd
	In no old R.L	Falsification	In H.B	In R.C
IP46; ; Voc; familiar-ity R.M only in 10 C. familiar BPV		Familiar-ity		do
IP46; 9ed		Family	; acs large hook ...	do
small hook Voc	In no old R.L	Fanciful		do
	In no old R.L except Gra' 54 Fantastical	Fantastic-al-ly	In H.B with one form ...	In R.C do
Voc. BP do.		Fashionable	See for-ble ...	do. 3d p do
IP Voc	In no old R.L	Fastidious		
"	"	Fastidiousness	fastid' ...	do
	"	Favorable	contracted	Contracted
IP216	In no old R.L	Fault		
"	"	Faulty	i.e. fault'	i.e. fault'

Voc In no old R.L Feature ie feat' do

LP'46; Park; ged; wanting Nature }

wanting wanting " wanting Futurity } ie fut' do

LP'46; In no old R.L February do

Financial reform Financial do
In no old Rep. List of Reporting word-signs and contractions in Reporting ex p. 31

Voc In no old R.L Flexible }

" " Flexibility } ble bility do

LP'46; ged; never made a wordsign Follow }

" " " Following } do

LP'46; ged " Followed do

Voc. In no old R.L. Footstep ie footst'. ie footstep

Voc " Forge fōge do

" Forged, would be do

Never contracted Form }

" Formed }

Conform-ed wanting

Conformable ie conform + b do

BP Inform }

In no old R.L. Informed }

Informant } ie infor' + in 1st p to disting. it from Uniform do

Form &c continued.

Remarks	Word	Note
In no old R.L but Graham's p.119	Deform	
"	Deformed	do
In no old R.L	Deformity	i.e. defor'
; Ged.	Reform	
"	Reformed	Refor'
wanting; probably	Reformatory	one cont^n for the three words.
; Ged; B.P. do	Perform	
; " "	Performed	
; " ; B.P.	Performance	
In no old R.L	Transform	
"	Transformed	i.e. trasfor'
"	Transformation	do.
Voc "	Platform	
I.P.46 In no other old R.L	Former	
" "	Formerly	Both words alike
I.P.46; word-sign in Ged.	Found	
Not a word-sign in Ged. Not in B.P.U.	Founded	i.e. found' — do. See 1st l.
I.P.46 "	Foundation	
B.P.		

Voc. In no old R.L Fragment
" " " " " Fragmentary

In no old R.L Frank In H.B. In R.C
" " " " Frankly " "

Voc In no old R.L Frantic
" " " " Franticness } i.e. fratic' do { Frantic Franticaly
Frantically would be

I P'46. & B.P.'54 Frequency -cy omitted fre'n -cy omitted
I P'46 In no other old R.L Fruition Frushon[3] do
I P'46 Voc. & G.C. Full } do
wanting " G.C. Not in B.P.V. Fully }
I P'46; J. Park; Ged; 10ed Future } i.e. fut' in 1st l. do
wanting; wanting; " "; wanting B.P.V. Futurity }

G.

I P'46, Park, & Pat; B.P.'54 Ged; 10ed Gave do
Ged. Gaveit wd be do
by the general prin. of p107, R.4
Voc Not in Rep '46 Not in B.P.V. Geography
" Park " Geographical }
" ; wanting " Geographer }
I P'46 Ged Park Glorious do
Glory Glorious Not in B.P.V.

Pat, 9ed; Park, 10ed	Govern		
" " " "	Governed		do
Pat & B.P. "	Government		
In no old R.L	Governmental		
		contracted	do
9ed probably, 10ed. Not in B.P.V.	Governor	gov'or	do
In no old R.L. Not in Voc.	Grandchild		do 3^d p
Voc. In no old R.L.	Granddaughter		do 3^d p
" "	Grandson		do 3^d p
I.P.'46 & 9ed	Guilt		do
" "	Guilty		

H.

Park only	Had it		do
Never made a word-sign, but becomes one in Standard Phonography, because the analogous form would be ..., Not in B.P.V.	Halve	as shown by Halved	do
Never made a word-sign Not in B.P.V	Halved	Vet[3]	do
Never made a wordsign	Ofit	Vet[1]	do
P.P. I.P.'46; Park Not in B.P.V. have had only	Have had / Have it	Vet[2]	
In no old R.L	Hand in hand	p.129 2^d p	
In no old R.L, nor in Voc. Not in B.P.V.	Happiest		do.

) In no old R.L.	Has there	) Zeedher[3]	do 2d p
) Park; . B.P. do	Was there	) Zeedher[2]	do
) In no old R.L.	Is there	) Zeedher[1]	do
Park Not in B.P.V.	Have had		do
In no old R.L.	Have it		do
for Have not cautioned against by I.P. in '46 as liable to be confounded with Find. Mentioned by no other author preceding the H.B. Park Com. Phon. p 13 '49 B.P.V.	Have not	"when is not better"	" when more convenient."
I.P. '46; Voc Not in B.P.V.	Hazard		
" ; " "	Hazarded		do
" ; " "	Hazardous		
Voc. In no old R.L.	Henceforth		
I.P. '46 & Voc & B.P. '54 — but not made a w.s	Herein		do
Voc In no old R.L.	Hieroglyph		
"	Hieroglyphic	i.e. hieroglyph.	
Not in Voc "	Hieroglyphical		do
I.P. '46; Pat. Not in GC. Voc	Highlands	p 197	do
Pat. GC.	Island		
GC	Land		do

Notes	Word	Remarks	
SP '46 & Voc B.P.	Hitherto	Read. & Ex p 23	do
Not in Voc. In no old R.L.	Holier	would be full form	do
" "	Holiest	would be full form	do
Voc "	Holiness	would be full form	do
Park. In no old R. List. Vee-hook added to half length, that is, to pt for "hope to"	Hope to have	Have added by a Vee hook to hope. To being implied by § 250, 2.	do
In no old R.L.	Hypocrisy	In the H.B.	In R.C.
In no old R.L.	Hypocrite	hypocrit?	do
"	Hypocritical		

I

Notes	Word	Remarks	
Voc In R.M. only, p 114	Identical-ly	idéntical	do
Voc In no old R.L.	Identification		
R.M. p 35	Idolator	p 196	do
	Idolatry		
Voc	Ignominy	p 28 Writ Ex. near the bot.	do
Voc. In no old R.L. but Graham's (R.M. p 21)	Illegal		do
B.P.	Illegality		
Voc & B.P.	Illegible		
Voc & B.P.	Illegibility		wanting

Voc R.M. p21 & Not in B.P.V.	Illegitimate	Illegit'	Illegitimat' notwithstanding there is but one t in Illegitimacy
" "	Illegitimacy		
Voc	Illiberal	i.e. lbrl	i.e. lbrl.
I.P.'46 " ; P.P.	Illiberality		
Voc In no old R.L.	Illogical		
wanting "	Illogicalness		wanting
Voc In no old R.L.	Imaginable	'aginab'	do
I.P.'46 & Voc Not in B.P.V.	Imagine	'agin'	
" "	Imaginary		do
" "	Imagination		
Not in Voc. In no old R.L.	Imagined	'agined	do
Voc In no old R.L.	Immeasurable		do
	Immigrate		do
	Immigrated		
Not in B.P.V.	Immoral	mrl	mrl
	Immorality		See under Moral-ity
I.P.'46 & Voc & 9 (B.E.)	Immortality	cs	
In no old R.L.	Immortalise	Immort- by Mist-	do
In no old R.L.	Impassionate		Cont^d ... do; full form w^d have been shorter, viz.

Voc	In no old R.L.	Imperceptible	}	
"	"	Imperceptibility	}	wanting
Voc	In no old R.L.	Implacable	}	do
wanting	"	Implacability	}	
Voc	In no old R.L.	Impoverish	}	
	"	Impoverished	}	Sh dotted
Voc.	"	Impoverishment	}	wanting
2d p; Pat; & B.P.	Ged & Park	Impracticable	}	do
2d p	Pat & B.P. wanting	Impracticability	to distinguish it from impractical	
	in Ged was Impracticable not in B.P.V.	Impractical, dws,		do
	In no old R.L.	Impregnate	}	do
	"	Impregnated	}	wanting
	"	Impregnable	i.e. impreg'	do
	"	Impregnation	}	wanting
	In no old R.L.	Improper	}	
	"	Improperly	impro'	improp'
	"	Impropriety	one form for the three words.	
BPV	in consideration	"In (the) Consideration"	"In (the) consideration"	1st l. "In (or in the) Consideration"

; B.P. do	Inaccuracy, drs.		
; B.P. do	Inaccurate, drs.		do
Voc In no old R.L.	Inauspicious		
" "	Inauspiciously		do
" "	Inauspiciousness		not given
I.P. 46 1st p.a	Incline	1st p	do
" 2d p.a Not in B.P.V.	Inclination	inclin.	
Voc In no old R.L.	Incombustible		do
"	Incombustibility		
Voc	Inconsiderable		do
wanting B.P.	Inconsiderableness		wanting
Voc In no old R.L.	Incredible		
" "	Incredibility		
In no old R.L.	Indescribable		
R.M.	Indication		do
"	Induction		do
Voc Not in G.C. Not in B.P.V.	Indignity		do
" G.C.	Indignant		
" " " 2d p	Indignation		

Voc. R.M only — Indivisible ⎫
In no old R.L. Indivisibility ⎭ ....

Voc; In no old R.L. Indoctrinate ⎫
wanting; Indoctrinated ⎬ .... do
; Indoctrination ⎭

⎫ Inevitable .... distinguished do
⎬ ged. distinguished by outline — by position from unavoidable
⎭ Unavoidable .... do

, In no old R.L. "Inexperience, in (the) experience" do
inexperience in the experience — See, et l. as to form of arrangement

In no old R.L. Inexperienced In-Sprenst? do

Voc. In no old R.L. Inferential
i.e. infer + En-hook .... do
Voc. In no old R.L. Inference

Voc — R.P. Inferior ⎫
" — " Inferiority ⎭ one sign for the two words

I P.46, Voc. In no old R.L. aft '46 Infinite ⎫
wanting; " " Infinity ⎭ i.e. nft — i.e. nfnt?

Voc. In no old R.L. Infinitesimal-ly
i.e. Infinite + Es .... do
Voc. In no old R.L. Infinitude

Voc " Infirm ⎫
" " Infirmity ⎭ one sign for both words

	B.P. 2d p.	Inform		
	"	Informed	1st p.	
	Not in B.P.	Informant	i.e. infor'	i.e. infor'
In no old R. L.		Uniform		
		Uniformity	3d p. i.e. unifor'	3d p. do
Voc.	"	Informality	contracted	do
I P 46; 9 ed. + B.P.	Not in 10 ed	Information		do
In no old R. L.		Infringe	Infringe	
		Infringed	Infringed	
		Infringer		
		Infringement	Infringement	
I P 46; 9 ed	Not in B.P.V	Inquire		do
" "	"	Inquiry	i.e. in'wer	
" "	"	Inquired, d'en,		do
I P 46 Park	Not in B.P.V	Inscribe		do
	"	Inscribed		
In no old R. L.		Insecure		do
I P 46 + 9 ed.		Insecurity		
or		Insolence	by rules of H. B	do
; B.P. do.		Insolent would be		do

Shorthand notes	Word	Outline	Remarks
Voc In no old R.L.	Insolvency		tho' Solvency is
	Insolvent would be		do
Voc; Park only / Not in B.P.V	Inspect		
" wanting "	Inspected		i.e. Inspect-d notwithstanding there is no t sound in Inspec
" wanting "	Inspection		
In no old R.L.	Instinctive In H.B. & Cont^d		In R.C. & Contracted
; Park only Not in B.P. Voc	Instruct		do
"	Instructed		
I.P.46, Park, & R.M., & B.P but not "in (the) construction"	"Instruction, in (the) construction"		"Instruction, in (or in the) Construction"
In no old R.L.	Instructive-ly (p.168, R.5)		do
"	Instructiveness		wanting
; sometimes. In no old R.L.	Instructor		do
	Insular		Do. as to use of In-hook
or	Insulate (by rules of H.B.)		
or	Insulation		
Voc	Insult		do
"	Insulted (By rules of H.B. p.168, R.8)		
Distinguished by outline (B.P. 2^d p.)	Insuperable	Distinguished by Position	
Not in B.P.V	Inseparable		

or	In no old R.L	Intelligible / Intelligibility	one form in H.B.	Do. in R.C
	Not in B.P.V.	Intercession		
	In no old R.L	Intermingle / Intermingled	-cession added by Iss-Eshon	do / wanting
IP46	Ged; B.P.	Interpret / Interpreted / Interpretation	2d p. acc. to accented vowel	do. 1st p
	In no old R.L	Intestate		do
Voc	In no old R.L	Intimidate / Intimidated / Intimidation	i.e. intimid'	do
Voc.	In no old R.L	Intolerable	i.e. intol'	intoler'
	In no old R.L	Intrinsic / Intrinsically		wanting
	In no old R.L.	Introspection		
Voc	In no old R.L	Invent / Invented / Inventor	i.e. invent'	do

IP46; Ged. B.P. (large hook)	Invention		do
Not in B.P.V.	Invert	See Part V. p. 8. R 1	do
"	Inverted		
R.M	Investigation	R.C.	Phr.-B
Voc. In no old R.L	Invisible		
"	Invisibility		
IP46; B.P. In no old R.L	Invite	p. 168. R. 8	do
wanting "; Not in B.P.V	Invited		
" "; Not in B.P.V.	Invitation		
Voc. Not in B.P.V.	Involve	p. 168. R. 8	do
"	Involved		
IP46; Park. Voc. Not in B.P.V.	Irrational		
" ; B.P.	Rational		
Voc. In no old R.L	Irrecoverable		do
Voc. In no old R.L	Irreligion		do
" "	Irrelegious		do
Ged; B.P. do.	Irrespective-ly		
Not in G.C.; B.P.	Respective-ly		do
IP46 G.C.; B.P.	Irresponsible		do
" wanting; wanting	Irresponsibility		

Note	Word	Reference	
	Is a-n § 71		do
	As a-n		do
In no old R.L	Is said § 71		do
"	Has said	p 167. R. 1; p 182, R. 4.	do
In no old R.L	Is said to have		do
In no old R.L	Is there)	Zeedher[1]	do
"	Has there)	Zeedher[3]	) 2d p
Park and B.P.	Was there)	Zeedher[2]	do
Not in B.P.V	Issued		do
"	It had	Ted[3]	do
Ted[2] Park, generally; B.P. do.	It would	"	do
A + B only; generally	It ought	Tet[1]	do
In no old R.L	It had not	Tent[3]	do
Tent[2], Park; S.P. + B.P.	It would not	"	do
In no old R.L	It ought not	Tent[1]	do
"	It not	Tent[2]	do
In no old R.L	It ought to have	Tef[1]	do
R. M. 54. Not in B.P.V.	It would have	Tef[3]	do
S.P. 10 ed.	Whatever	Tef[2]	do

In no old R.L	It ought to have had	l	do
"	It would have had	l	do
Park '52 In no old R.L	It will have	l	do
"	It will have had	l	do
Park & Pat 2d p	It would		do
R.M only, '54 Adm B.P.V	It would have		do
In no old R.L	It would have had	l	do
Park ; B.P. 2d p	It would not		do

J.

IP46. In no later R.L	Jehovah	l	do 2d p
	Jove	l	wanting
Ged. In no old R.L	Juvenile		by
IP46 & A&B'50; BP'54	Jesus	l	do in first list
IP46 & Reed '55; Ged & BP; Pat '50	Jesus Christ		do
In no old R.L	Jesus of Nazareth	contracted	contracted
In no old R.L	Judicature-ory		
In no old R. List	Judiciary	In H.B.	In R.C.
	Judiciously		

I P'46; Park '49. B.P. In no later R List	Jurisdiction	contracted	contracted
I P'46 & Ged. & B.P	Jury		do
" (gentlemen of the Jury)			
	Juryman, -dwrs		do
In no old R.L.	Justifiable	omitting -ble	
I P'46; B.P. do	Justification		do / do in 1st list
Voc. In no old R.L.	Juxtaposition		do

K.

I P'46 & Ged, & B.P	Kingdom of Christ		do
" " & B.P.	Kingdom of God		do

L.

In no old R.L	Languish	lang'wish	do
Voc "	Legendary	leg'ё'dary	do
In no preceding R.M list but Graham's & afterward B.P	Legislature		do
Voc In no old R.L	Lexicography	contracted	do
" "	Lexicographer		
Voc In no old R.L	Libertinism		do 2d p
	Longer	; cs	do
Voc. In no old R.L	Looking-glass	or	

M.

I P'46 In no other old R.L	Machinery	machi'ry	do

In no old R.L.	Machinist	mach'st	do
In no old R.L.	Magnet-ic		do
In no old R.L.	Magnetism	contracted	do
9ed. & B.P.; Park	Majesty	3d p acc'g to vowel	do. 2d p
" wanting wanting	Majestic		
In no old R.L.	Malevolent	large-hook	do
In no old R.L.	Malformation	large hook	contracted
Voc In no old R.L.	Malicious	contracted	
"	Maliciously	maliah'	do
"	Maliciousness		wanting
B.P. do	Malignant	malig'	do
I.P. 46; 9ed. & B.P. Not in 10ed.	Material		do
" " "	Immaterial	§ 239, R 4, &c	do
Not in B.P.V.	Materialism	; cs	do
; I.P. 10 ; et p	Matter		do
; Park only without position	Maybe		do

IP46 ; Park ; B.P	Measure		do
; Park. ; B.P full length	Measured		do
IP46 In no other old R.L	Mechanic		
"	Mechanical		
In no old R.L	Mechanism		
Voc. In no old R.L	Mediterranean		
IP10 . In no other old R.L	Meeting		do
2d p IP46. In no other old R.L	Melancholy	large hook	
Small hook B.P ; B.P do 2d p.	Melioration		do
" do 2d p	Amelioration		do
R.M. mental	Mental-ity	R.C	Phr. B.
IP46 In no other old R.L.	Merchandise	merchadise	do
Voc In no old R.L	Messenger	mess'ger	do
Voc. In no old R.L	Merciful	mer	
In no old R.L	Metaphysical		
In no old R.L	Method		do 1st p.
	Methodical	2d p	
Voc In no old R.L	Methodist		
	Methodistic		do
	Methodistical	methodist	

Notes	Word	
Voc. In no old R.L.	Metropolitan	IP in C.
" "	Metropolis	do
In no old R.L.	Microscope	
	Microscopic	
; B.P.	Mightiest, ders,	do
; B.P. do	Mightiness, ines,	do
B.P.	Million	
Not in B.P.V.	Millionth	large hook
Voc. In no old R.L.	Minimum ; cs	do
; B.P.	Minority minorit'	do
Not in B.P.V. nor any other old R.L.	Misconjecture	do
"	Misconjectured mis'jec'	
Not in B.P.V.	Conjecture-d	(?) do
Voc. In no old R.L.	Misfortune 'jec	do
" "	Modification	
IP'46	Monstrous	
"	Monstrosity	dotted
" & Ged. & B.P.	Moral	
" " ; B.P.	Morality	moral' moral' See Immoral-ity

Mortal-ity See Immortal-ity

ged	Mortgage	
In no old R.L.	Mortgagee	
In no old R.L.	Mortification; cs.	
In no old R.L.	Much will	do
"	Much will have	do

N.

Voc. In no old R.L	Needful	do
Park; ged	Neglect } 2d p. neg	
"	Neglected	
Voc In no old R.L. Not in B.P.	Negligent } 2d p. negl	do 1st p.
"	Negligence	
Voc In no old R.L	New Foundland	do
In no old R.L.	No other	do
"	No other one	do
"	Nomenclature	do 1st p.
"	Noncompliance Read. Ex. p. 21	do
Voc "	Nondescript	
" "	Nonessential	do
Northern States R.H Nor' for North	North America	

		North Carolina	
In no old R. L.		Northeast — East by a loop	do
"		Northeastern ; cs — in analogy with Southeastern	
R. M. p 123, line 162		Northwest — in analogy with Southwest	do
R. M. western states		Northwestern — in analogy with Southwestern	do
	In no old R. L	Nourish	
		Nourishment	do

O.

	In no old R. L	Objectionable — p 96. R. 3	do
	Not in B. P. V.	Objective — With T or hook to distinguish certainly from Objection	
	In no old R. L	Observant	do
		Observance	wanting
	In no old R. L	Obstruct	
		Obstructed — Distinguished from Abstract-ed by position	do
	O Park Not in B. P. V.	Obstruction	
large loop	Never made a word sign	Of it — See Have had, &c.	do
;	B. P. do	Of thr	do
;	Not in B. P. V.	Of their own	do
	In no old R. L	Officious	
	"	Officiousness	

[shorthand] Voc.	In no old P. L.	Oftentimes	[shorthand] contracted	[shorthand] do
[shorthand] "	"	Ofttimes	[shorthand]	[shorthand]
[shorthand]	Not in B.P.V. nor any other old R.L.	Old and New Testament	[shorthand] cont. and omitted	[shorthand] do
[shorthand] I.P.46	Not in B.P.V.	Old Testament	[shorthand] contracted	[shorthand] do
[shorthand] on	B.P. [shorthand]	On either hand	[shorthand] 'either'and	do
[shorthand] on	B.P. do.	On the other hand	[shorthand] 'other'and	do
[shorthand] I.P.46; ged [shorthand] on	B.P. do	On the one hand	[shorthand] 'one'and	do
[shorthand] I.P.46; small hook	[shorthand] = wn in ged. Not in B.P.V. (= only " "	Only	[shorthand] large hook	do
	Not in B.P.V.	Only as	[shorthand] large hook	do
[shorthand] Voc.	B.P. do	Onward / Inward	[shorthand] [shorthand]	do
[shorthand] "				
[shorthand] Voc.	Not in B.P.V.	Organic	[shorthand]	do
Not in Voc.	Not in B.P.V.	Ornamentation	[shorthand] orn'ashon	[shorthand] in full
[shorthand], [shorthand] Voc.	Not in B.P.V.	Ostentatious-ly	[shorthand] p. 193. R. 3	[shorthand] ostentatiousness not given
[shorthand]	"	Ostentatiousness		
[shorthand]	Not in B.P.V. nor any other old R.L.	Over it	[shorthand]	do

P.

[shorthand] Voc.	Not in B.P.V. nor any other old R.L.	Paganism	[shorthand] pāg'ism	do
[shorthand] "	"	Painful	[shorthand] painf'	do
in full [shorthand], [shorthand]	Not in B.P.V.	Parallel-ed	[shorthand] parall'	[shorthand] [shorthand] large hook for L first explained in the Hand Book

Voc Not in B.P.V. nor any other [old R.L]	Partial-ly	partial'	do
" ; B.P.V.	Partiality		
IP216 and Voc Not in B.P.V.	Party		do
Not in B.P.V.	Party of the first part	pä'	do
"	Party of the second part		do
Voc. Not in B.P.V. nor any other old R.L.	Passenger	pasiger	do
IP46; Voc & B.P.V.	Passionate		do 3p.
Not in B.P.V.	Patent		
"	Patented		Pr. & p. tense alike
or or Not in B.P.V.	Patentable		HB sign for ble
or Not in B.P.V. Not in any other old R.L.	Paternal		HB sign for nl
Voc Not in B.P.V. nor any other old R.L.	Pedant	pedant'	do
" "	Pedantic		
" "	Pedantry	pedä'try	do
Not in B.P.V. nor any other old R.L.	Peevish	peevish'	do
"	Peevishly		
"	Peevishness		
Voc. "	Penetrable	pent'b	
" "	Penetrability		penetrate i.e. with two t-sounds

	Not in B.P.V	Penetrate	pent'rate	penetrate
	"	Penetrated		
	Voc. "	Penitential		
	P46 B.P.V do	Perfect		
	" "	Perfected	to distinguish Perfected from Perfect	
	Not in B.P.V	Pernicious	p 193. R.3	
	"	Perniciously		
	P46; Pat; B.P.do Voc	Perpetual		do
	wanting, Not in B.P.V. "	Perpetuate		
	" ; " "	Perpetuation		
	Not in B.P.V.	Personification	person-fa'shon	do
	B.P	Perspective	See Retrospective and Prospective	
	Not in B.P.V.	Perspicuity		DO.
	Not in B.P.V	Pertinacious		
	"	Pertinaciously		
	"	Pertinaciousness		not given
	Voc. & Park. Not in B.P.V	Pestilential	contracted	do
	Not in B.P.V	Philosophy		do.
	B.P do	Philosophic		
	Not in B.P.V.	Philosophical		

Not in B.P.V	Photography		Photograph
"	Photographic		Photographic
"	Photographist		
"	Photographer		
I.P.46; Yed ; B.P. do	Plaintiff ...		do 1st p
Not in B.P.V	Platform		
I.P.46 and Voc. Not in B.P.V	Plenty		
" " "	Plentiful	plnt ...	do
Not in B.P.V or any other old R.L	Polygamy		Polygamy
"	Polygamous		Polygamist
I.P.46; 2d p Pat, Park do; B.P do	Popular		
wanting; 2d p ... " " ; ... B.P ... Ting ed.	Popularity	1st p. the better to distinguish from Public, &c ...	do
I.P.46 + Yed; A+B; B.P	Possess		
" " ; "	Possessed	p. 61, R. 8	do.
Not in B.P.V	Possesses, Ers,		do
	Possessive		do
	with the 1st l. of Rep. Comp. under P.	compare 1st list of Hand Books	
Voc. Not in B.P.V or any other old R.L	Possessor,		do
I.P.46; Voc. Not in B.P.V.	Possibilities		

B.P. Possible-y

P46; Voc; B.P. Possibility

Park; B.P. (povert) Poverty — pov — do

Not in B.V. Hope to have — do

P46 Pat 50; B.P.; Voc Practicable

" " "; " Practicability — do

P46; Pat. do B.P.; gel Practice

wanting; wanting; "; Practical-ly — do

" ; " "; ged Practiced — do

P46 + ged Not in B.P.V Precipitate

" " " Precipitated — precipit.

" " " Precipitation

; Voc Not in B.P.V Predestinate

; " " Predestinated — pr + p.t alike

; " " Predestination

Not in B.P.V Predominate

Em-stroke " Predominated — Em hook in both

" Predomination — wanting

IP 216 ; Voc. ; B.P Prejudice
" " " Prejudiced
" " " Prejudicial

IP 46 ; B.P Prepare do
" Prepared do
IP 46 " Preparation
Not in B.P.V. nor any other old R.L. Prerogative.
P.V.; Not in B.P.V Presbytery
" B.P.V Presbyterian presbyt Tho' there is no n in the 1st word
B.P.V Prescribe do
" Prescribed contracted
" Prescription do
" Present do
Not in B.P.V Presented present'
" Presentation
Park only. Not in B.P.V. Presidential contracted do
do
Voc. Not in B.P. Voc. Priestcraft do
Not in B.P.V nor any other R.L Primogeniture do
infull. Not in B.P.V. nor any other old Reporting List Problematical do

Note	Word	Remarks	
Not in B. P. V	Proclaim		
"	Proclaimed		
"	Proclamation	contracted	do
		See Declaim and Exclaim	
Voc. "	Prodigious		
SP 46 & Voc. B. P. V.	Production	produshon	do.
Not in B. P. V	Productive		do
"	Productiveness	Prod'	wanting
Not in B. P. Voc and not in SP 10	Profit		
"	Profited		do
"	Profitable		
Not in B. P. V nor any other old R L	Prognosticate		
"	Prognosticated		
"	Prognostication	prog	prognost'
Not in B. P. V	Promulgate		
"	Promulgated	H. B. large El-hook	
"	Promulgation	No t - sound in Promulgation	
B. P. V	Proper		
"	Properly		
SP 46 "	Property	prop'	do

Not in B.P.V nor in I.P. 10	Prophet	do.
"	Prophetic	do.
Voc Not in B.P.V.	Propitious	
"	Propitiousness	wanting
I.P. 216; Jul, B.P. do (r not omitted)	Proportionate	(r omitted)
B.P; B.P; Not in B.P.V	Propriety / Proper-ly / Impropriety	Propriety See Proper-ly
B.P.V	Proscribe	do
Not in B.P.V	Proscribed	See Prescribe-d, 1st p.
B.P.V	Proscription	2d p. in analogy with Prescription p. 193, R. 3 — do
Not in B.P.V	Proscriptive	in analogy with Prescriptive p. 193, R. 3. — do
; Park 2d p. Not in B.P.V	Prospect	
; " prob. "	Prospected	1st p. — do. See p. 3, Exercise on Logographs
, ; B.P.V.	Prospective-ly	do. 2d p.
I.P. 246; Voc; B.P.	Prosperity	by p. 118, R. 4; 'perity joined — do
Voc; Park; Not in B.P.V	Prostitute	
" perhaps "	Prostituted	do.
I.P. 46; Voc. Not in B.P.V	Protestant	do.
wanting; "	Protestantism	

Voc Not in B.P. Provincial

Park Not in B.P.V. Punctual
" Punctuality
to delete

Not in B.P.V nor any other old R.d. Pusillanimous
" Pusillanimity

Q.

Voc. Not in B.P.V nor any other old R.d. Qualification
" " Questionable
H.B. sign for -ble

R.

I.P.46 B.P. do Rapid
" " Rapidity
rapid

repeat" repeated B P do Repeat-ed
repeat
do

Not in B.P.V. Repute-d-ation
repute
do

I.P.46; Voc, B.P.; I.P.10 Ray Ray Rather
If Ray-Ray then old. See H.B. p 130, § 264 for lengthening of straight lines to add Thr.

Rather than
by p. 97, R.8
Than added by En hock

Voc. Not in B.P.V Ratification

B.P.V. Rational-ly-ity
contracted
do

Not in B.P.V. Irrational-ly-ity
contracted
do

IP46; Park. Not in B.P.V	Real }		
" ; " "	Really }		do
IP46; Ged Not in B.P.V	Rule }		do
(?) " " "	Ruled }	H.B. large L-hook	
IP46; Voc; Park " (Small hook 3rd position)	Reality	1st p. tho' the accented vowel is third place	
IP46 Voc Not in B.P. Voc (2d p, 2d p)	Realization	drs. 1st p strictly 2d p. p149, R2	do
IP46; Voc; Park "	Realise,		do
" ; " " "	Realised	drs.	do.
Not in B.P.V nor any other old R.L	Rebutting evidence		
Not in BPV. nor in any other old R.L	Recapitulate }		
"	Recapitulated }		do
"	Recapitulation }	recapit'	
IP46 "	Recollect }		
"	Recollected }		
" "	Recollection }	See Collect-ed	
"	Recover }		
"	Recovered }		do
"	Recovery }	recov'	
"	Recoverable }		

Voc. Not in B.P.V. nor in any other old R.L. Redundance-cy. contracted --- do

" " Redundant-ly

I.P.46 & Voc; 96 & B.P.V. Reform-ed

Voc. Not in B.P.V. nor any other old R.L. Reformatory

I.P.46. Pat & Park do. 96 & B.P. Reformation

Voc. Not in B.P.V. nor any other old R.L. Refractory do 2d p.

B.P. do Regard

" Regarded §269,3 do Present & past tense alike

" Regret

" Regretted do Present and past tense alike

Not in B.P.V. nor any other old R.L. Regenerate

" Regenerated

" Regenerative

Not in B.P.V. nor any other old R.L. Reject

" Rejected

" Rejection i.e. reject tho' there is no t - sound in Rejekshon.

; Park small hook B.P.V. Relate

" " Related

Voc. ; B.P.V. Relation

" Park small hook ; B.P.V. Relative

	Not in B.P.V.	Relevancy		do
; Park ; "		Relief, Relieve	relevan?	do
ged. Voc.	Not in B.P.V nor in any other old R.L	Religionist		do
	Not in B.P.V. nor in any other old R.L	Generalized		do
Voc.	9 C + B.P	Relinquish		
"	" Not in B.P.V	Relinquished		do
"	Not in B.P.V nor in any other old R.L	Relinquishment		
I.P.'46;	9 ed. small hook Not in B.P.V	Reluctant-ly		
wanting "	"	Reluctance	reluct?	
I.P.'46 + 9 ed.	Not in B.P.V	Remit		
"	"	Remitted		do
" "	"	Remittance	remit?	
Voc.	Not in B.P.V nor any other old R.L	Remonstrate		
"	"	Remonstrated		
	Not in B.P.V	Repeat		do
	"	Repeated		
	"	Repetition		
		Rapidity		
; B.P; wanting		Repute-ed-ation		do

IP'46 & 9ed. Not in BPV Repent. } do
" " " Repented }
" " " Repentance } repent'

Not in BPV nor in any other old R.L. Replenish } do
" Replenished }
" Replenishment } replen'

" Reprehensible }
" Not in I.P.Voc. Reprehensibility } reprens' H.B sign for -ble-bility
" Reprehensive }
" Reprehension } repren' wanting

IP'46; Voc. BPV Representatives Representative with Tive-hook to clearly distinguish it from Representation. H.B plan of adding -ive in some cases.

IP'46 & Pat BPV Republican With Enhook the better to distinguish it from related words. do

Voc. Not in B.P.V. nor 9e RM Repugnant } do
Voc " wanting Repugnance } repug'

BPV Repute } do
Not in BPV Reputed }
" Reputation } reput'

Not in BPV nor any other old R.L	Reserve			
"	Reserved			
"	Reservation	contracted Reservation	contracted	
Voc; Ged Rs; BP	Respect			
" " "BPV	Respected		do	
" Not in BPV	Respecting			
" "	Respectful	resp'		
Not in BPV	Respectable		do	
Voc. "	Respectability			
BPV	Respective-ly		do	
Voc. Not in BPV	Resplendent			
" "	Resplendence	resplend'		
IP'46; Ged; BPV	Respond			
" Not in BPV nor any other R.L	Responded		do	
wanting " "	Respondent			
wanting " "	Respondence	respond'		
Voc. Not in BPV nor any other old R.L	Responsive			
IP'46 + Pat + Park + Ged. + BPV	Responsible			
" " " " "	Responsibility			

N-B sign for ble, -bility.

Not in B.P.V. nor in any other old R.L.		Restrict		
"		Restrict		Pr. & p. tense alike
"		Restriction		do
"		Restrictive		do
"		Retract		
"		Retracted		
"		Retraction		retract' though retrak-shon has but one t-sound
Park.'49; 9ed ; BP		Retrospect		do.
wanting "	" wanting	Retrospection	retrosp'	
	" ; B.P.do.	Retrospective	retrosp'v	do
Not in BPV nor in any other old R.L.		Revenge		do
"		Revenged	reve'j	

Error in H-B Revenged Should have been given separately with as its form. Same error in Rep. Comp.

"		Revengeful		do
"		Revengefulness		wanting
Voc.	Park.'49. Not in 9C nor in BPV	Reverential	reveren'-	do
SP46	Not in B.PV	Revolve		
"	"	Revolved	riv'	riv'

Not in R.P.1 nor any old R.L. Rhetor

IP'46; ... BP. Rhetoric

" " Not in BPV Rhetorical

Not in BPV nor any other old R.L. Roman Catholic — See Catholic do

" Roman Catholicism — See Catholic do

IP'46 R.M. BP do Ruined do.

" RM BP do Renewed do.

" ged Park'49 Not in BPV Rule — Ruled do

" " " Real-ly do

IP'46; Park'49; ged. Not in BPV. Ruler do

S

Not in BPV nor in any other old R.L. Saddens do

" Said to have do

IP'46; Voc NOT IN BPV Sanctify — Sanctified — Sanctification — Sanct wanting

Qualification
Modification
Ratification

IP'46; Voc. Not in BPV Sanguinary ... do

" "; Park " Sanguine ... do

IP46; Voc. RM. BPV 3d p. Savior ... do

Sceptical. See Skeptic-al

Scepticism See Skepticism

IP'46; Voc. BP. do 2d p. School ... do

" ; " Scale ... do

" ; " Skill ... do

Voc Not in BPV nor in any other old RL. Scoundrel ⎫ scou'drel do

" " Scoundrelism ⎭ scou'drelism

Not in B.P.V., nor any other old R.L. Seclude ... do

" Schooled ... do

" Secluded ... or ... p168, R8

IP'46. 2d p BPV 2d p Seclusion ... Shen hook.

BP do. Sectarian ...

Not in B.P.V Sectarianism

IP'46 Ged. " Secular ... l expressed by an El-hook

Voc. Not in B.P.V Sedentary

" " Legendary do

" " Pedantry do

	Not in B.P.V	Sensual	p 193. R 3	do
	B.P.V	Sensuality		
		Partial-ity		do
	Not in B.P.V nor any other old R L	Sentimentalism		
		Set off		do
		Set forth		do
	Park '49 Not in B.P.V	Shall it		do
		Wish it		do
		"She would, she had"	"She would, she had"	do
		She ought, wish it		do
		Significancy		
	Park — B.P	Signification		do
	Not in B.P.V nor any other old R. L	Significative	tive	
	SP46, Pat, Park, B.P	Significant		do
ged in full				
	B.P.V	Simple-y		do
	SP46 & 9 Ed. Not in B.P.V	Simplicity		
	In no old R.L	Simpler		do
		Simplest		do
in full		Simplification		do
		Simplified (deriv. contraction) See Simplify next page	Simp' fi-shon Simp' fied	do

Not in B.P.V nor in any other old R.L	Simplify			do
S.P.46 Ged Not in B.P.V	Sister	9		do
in full — Not in B.P.V	Skeptic			
in full — "	Skeptical			
"	Skepticism			
S.P.46; ged	Skill			do
" "	Scale			do
" " B.P. do	School			do
Not in B.P.V	Skilled			do
" Seclusion 2^d^ p	Schooled, Seclude			do
Not in B.P.V nor any other old R.L	Slumber	Slu'ber		
"	Sober-minded			do
"	Sober-mindedness			
"	Solvency	solven'		do
B.P.	Some one			do
Not in B.P.V nor any other old R.L	Some other			do
" "	Some other one		see 1st l.	do
Voe " "	South east	east pronounced Tho' South		do 2^d^ p
Voe " "	South eastern	es. 8		

Not in B.P.V. nor any of R.L.	Southwest	2d p acc'g to accented vowel; Sou'west	do 3d p
9th Voc. "	South western	Sou'wes'ern; 2d p. acc'g to the accented vowel	do 3d p
Voc. "	Southern	2d p. acc'g to accented vowel; Suthe'n	do 3d p. tho' South is given in the 2d p.
"	Southerner	i.e. Southe'ner acc'g to accented vowel	do 3d p.
in full "	Speakable		do
S.P.'46 Not in B.P.V.	Speaker		
"	Specify	specif'	do 2d p
"	Specific		
"	Speculate	speculat	do
	Speculated		
"	Speculator		
"	Speculatory		wanting
; ...+B.; "	Spendthrift		
Not in B.P.V. nor any other old list	Spiritualism		do 2d p
; B.P. 2d p	Spoken	Spō'n, 1st p. because of speak	do
Voc 2d p Not in B.P.V	Spontaneous	1st p	
"	Spontaneity	1st p. tho' accented vowel in 2d place for 1st word	wanting
S.P.'46 & Voc. B.P.V. only	"State (sometimes in phr.)"		do See 1st list under T
" & Voc; A.C. + B.P.	Stated		do
S.P.'46; Voc, R.M.; BPV	Constitute.d		do

IP46; ... ke; ... Park NOT Stenography
wanting ... ; wanting, IN Stenographic ... sten' ... do
" ... ; wanting, BPV Stenographer ... BP's May to June 18.. gives ... for Stenography; but ...
Voc. Not in BPV nor any other old R.L Stepping-stone ... do
BPV ... Strength
Not in BPV. would be ... Strengthen
BPV ... Strengthened
IP46 + God ... BPV Stupendous
wanting Stupendousness ... wanting
; God ... Not in B.P.V nor any other old R.L Subjective ... with ... hook to clearly distinguish it from ... Subjection
" Sublime
" Sublimity
Voc Not in 96 nor B.P.V, & Park Subserve ... do
" " " Subserved
IP46 ... 96 + B.P.V Subservient ... subser'
" " Subserviency
. Pat. Park, + BP do Substantial
wanting ——— Substantiality ... wanting ... distinguished from Substantiate d

Not in BPV nor any other old R.L.		Substantiate		
"		Substantiated		
"		Substantiation		
, BPV		Successful		See H.B. p. 194
Voc. in full	Not in B.P.V. nor any other old R.L.	Succinct-ly		
		Succinctness		wanting
A & B only; B.P. such an	Not in BPV	Such a one		do
JP 46 & Park	Not in B.P.V.	Such are		do
Not in B.P.V. nor any other old R.L.		Such had		do
"		Such had not		do
"		Such have		do
"		Such have had		do
"		Such ought		do
"		Such ought not		do
"		Such ought not to have		do
"		Such ought to have	p 129, § 250, 2.	do
"		Such ought to have had		do
"		Such were		do

Sub.

Park; Park. p. 16 N. B.P.V 2d p. only — Not in BPV — Such would — do

Not in B.P.V. — Such would have — do

" — Such would have had — do

" — Such would not — do

IP'46 Pat BP; Ged — Suggest

" " " " — Suggested — Pr. & p. tense alike

" " " " — Suggestion

Not in B.P.V nor any other old R.L — Suggestive-ly

" — Suggestiveness — i.e. Suggest + ive

in full

Not in B.P.V nor any other old R.L — Supererogation

" — Supererogatory — wanting

Voc — " — Superincumbent — do

IP'46 Ged do. — BPV — Superintend

" " — wanting — Superintended

" " — " — Superintendent

" " — " — Superintendence

IP'46 & Ged; — BPV — Superior

" " — " — Superiority

Voc. Not in B.P.V nor any other old R.L — Supernatural

Voc — " — Superstitious

" — " — Superstitiousness

Voc Not in B.P.V — Supplant — do
LP46
Voc — Supplication
IP46 ged — Supply — do
LP46, ged do, B.P.V — Support — do
" " wanting — Supported — p.197
IP46 + ged, BPV Supreme Court — Supreme — do as in Supreme Court
" " Not in B.P.V — Supremacy
Not in B.P.V nor in any other old R.L. — Supreme Being
ged B.P.V — Suppress — do
" wanting — Express — do
ged B.P.V — Surprise — do
IP46 ged B.P. do — Surrender — do
" " " — Surrendered — p.99, R.4; p.168, R.8
Voc Not in B.P.V nor any other old R.L — Surreptitious-ly — p.193, R.3
Voc — Surreptitiousness — wanting
Not in B.P.V nor any other old R.L. — Survive — do
" — Survived — survi'
" — Survivor — wanting
Not in B.P.V nor any other old R.L — Susceptible
" — Susceptibility

		Word		
Park. Not in B.P.V.		Suspect	Gur	Gur
"		Suspected		
I P 446 + Ged	"	Suspend		do
" "	"	Suspended	suspend'. p168. R.8	
	"	Suspense		do
	"	Suspension		do
Not in B.P.V nor any other old R.L		Suspicion	suspen'	
Not in B.P.V		Sustain		do
"		Sustained	See Consistency &c	do
		Consistent		do
Not in B.P.V nor in any other old R.L		Swindle		
"		Swindled	or	
"		Swindler		
Not in B.P.V nor any other old R.L.		Sympathetic		
"		Sympathetical-ly	in strict position	
BPV		System		do
BPV		Systematic		
"		Systematical	would be the same	
		Arithmetic-al		do
		Problematical		do

T.

	Not in B.P.V. nor any other old R.L.	Tangible		do
	"	Tangibility		
Voc	"	Tantamount		do
	"	Technical		
	"	Technicality		
	"	Telegraph		
	"	Telegrapher		wanting
	"	Telegraphic		
	"	Telescope		
	"	Telescopic	p 193, R. 3, "illustrate, &c. A double contraction	
	"	Microscopic		
	In one old R.L. Not in BPV	Tell it	By p 107, R. 4	do
	Not in B.P.V nor any other old R.L.	Temperament		do
	"	Temperamental		wanting
Park	B.P.V do	Temperate		do
"	"	Temperance	No claim made as to this form. These words put in simply to show the whole class of Temp-s	
I P 46; Pat do. BPV		Temperature	tmptr	do
	Not in BPV	Terminate		
	"	Terminated		wanting
	"	Termination		

Compare Predominate.

IP'46 Not in B.P.V. nor any other list after 1846	Testamentary	do
Not in B.P.V. nor any other old R.L.	Testify	
B.P.V. They had not	Than it, They wd not, They had not	do
Not in BPV nor any other old R.L	Then it	do
"	They ought not	do
Voc "	Thankful-ly	
" "	Thankfulness	
or "	The first	do
"	The other one[7]	do
or "	Then it	do
full form "	Thenceforward	do
IP'46 + Voc; RM ; BP do	Theology	do
" " ; " "	Theological	do
Not in B.P.V	Theoretical-ly	
Not in B.P.V	There had	do
(there would be) B.P.V.	There would	do
Not in B.P.V nor any other old R.L	There it	do
Not in B.P.V	There ought	do
	There had not — Dhrent[3]	do
IP'46 ; B.P.V	There would not — Dhrent[1]	do
Not in BPV	There ought not	do
BPV	On the other hand — Dhrend[2]	do
"	On either hand — Dhrend[1]	do

Not in B.P.V	There it	Dhret^2	do
"	There ought	Dhret^1	do
"	There ought not See There had not		do
(there'd be) B.P.V	There would		do
BP do	There would not See There had not		do
or — BEV	Thereto		do
"	Hitherto		do
Voc Not in B.P.V nor any other old R.L	Thermometer		
"	Thermometrical		wanting
BPV do.	They had	Dhed^3	do
Not in B.P.V nor any other old R.L	They would	Dhed^3	do
"	They ought	Dhet^1	do
or Pink "	Though it	Dhet^3	do
B.P. do	They had not	Dhent^3	do
Not in B.P.V nor any other old R.L	They would not	Dhent^3	do
"	Then it	Dhent[illegible]	do
"	They ought not	Dhent^1	do
"	They would [illegible]		do
or Pink only [illegible]	They would, they had, though it		do

Not in B.P.V	They ought not		do
or	Then it		do
	They would not		do
; B.P. do	They had not		do
or	Than it		do
Park. '49	They will not		do
Park p 12 Comp. Thou "	They would (See They had)		do
Not in B.P.V	They would not (See They had not)		do
; Park p 6N.d Not in BPV	Think it	Thought	do
Not in B.P.V	This is only	Large El-hook	do
"	This is really	Large El-hook	do
I.P. '46; Not in BPV Yed, the L-hook having been changed to W. Small El-hook	This only	Large El-hook	do
or Not in BPV nor any other 6/a R.L.	Thou wilt		do
"	Thou wilt not		do
; Park. Not in BPV.	They will not		do
; Park '49 p 6N.d "	Though it (See They had)		do
; Park, p 6N.d; BPV	Thousand	}	do
Not in BPV	Thousandth	}	
"	Through one		do 3 p
"	Thunder (See Thunderstorm)		do

Voc Not in B.P.V Timid }
" " Timidity } do

IP46; 96; RM; BPV To become do
Bx

Tolerance
Tolerant

Tolerate }
Tolerated } toler' } Pr + p. tense alike
Toleration }

Voc Not in BPV. Torpid }
" " Torpidity } torpid' do

" Tragedy } Tragic }
" Tragic } Tragical }
" Tragical° } traj' "Tragedy" } traj'

" Tranquil }
BPV. 2d p Tranquility } tranq' 3d p do

Voc Not in B.P.V. Transatlantic do

IP46 Not in B.P.V Transcend }
" Transcended }

P.46 Not in B.P.V — Transcendent } trāsen'ant' trabant'
Voc " — Transcendental — Transcendentalism
Compare Transatlantic, Transcend-ed, Transcendent-al-ism

P.46 & Qed Not in B.P.V — Transfer
" " — Transferred } trāsf. transf'

Not in B.P.V — Transfers
" — Transference } trāsfs transfs.

In the Hand Book "Transfers-ence" and the same in the Rep. Comp. indicates a wrong spelling of "Transference" i.e. with one and not two r's in 2nd syll.

Not in B.P.V nor in any other old R.L. — Transform
" — Transformed } trāsfor' transfor
" — Transformation

" — Transient trā'sient

" — Transparent
" — Transparency } trāspā wanting
n omitted from trans

" — Try to have do.
p.167. R1. near close.
Voc " — Twelve } Telf2 do
" " — Twelfth
" — It will have Telf2 do

	Remarks	Word	Notes	
	Not in B.P.V	'T would have (For It would have)		do
	"	'T would have had (For It would have had, which see)		do
	Not in B.P.V nor any other old R.L.	Typography		
	"	Typographer		wanting
	"	Typographic-al		

U.

	Remarks	Word	Notes	
	B.P. No apparent diff. of p.	Unavoidable		do
	"	Inevitable		do
Voc	Not in B.P.V nor any other old R.L.	Unceremonious		do
	"	Uncommon	p. 14, Read. Ex	do
	Not in I.P.V. "	Uncontradicted	p. 142, R. 5	'ict for icted
	& I.P. '46. "	Undecided-ly		do
	"	Undignified		do
	I.P. '46 & 9ed Not in B.P.V	Unfortunate	deriv. Cont.	
		Fortunate		
	"	Uniform		
	"	Uniformity	uni for 3d p.	do
	9 C "	Inform		
	" "	Informed		
	wanting "	Informant	in for 1st p.	do

Not in BPV nor any other old R.L.	Unimaginable	imaginab.	do
"	Unimagined	unimagined	do
IP'46, Pat do; BP. in full	Universality	'versal'	do
Not in BPV, nor any other old R.L	Universalism	'vers'm	'versalism
IP'46; 'vers Park; BPV in full	Universe	'verse	do
'versity IP'46; 'vers' Pat, Park do; BPV in full	University		do
Not in BPV	Unmeasurable		do
"	Immeasurable		do
Not in BPV nor in any other old R.L	Unmeasured		do
IP'46; ; 9ed , BP do	Unquestionable		H-e sec for -ble
Not in BPV nor in any other old R.L	Unquestioned		
1 voc Not in BPV	Unreal, dws,	p194, R.5	do
Not in BPV	Unruly, dws,		do
"	Unrecompensed		do
"	Unreconciled	p111, 16	do
"	Unrecoverable	derivative cont. p194, R.5	
	Recovered-y-able		do
or Not in BPV	Unseasonable, dws	See H.B p174, 2 H.B see for -ble	
or "	Unseasoned, dws,		

or — Not in BPV Unsecured ... do

" Unseemly ... do

I.P. 46 & 9 ed " Unspeakable, §174, 2 ... do
tho' ... was 'speak' deriv. contⁿ p 194, R. 5

or Unsurmountable ... do
See Writᵍ Ex. §42, 1(a) §174, 2 Bee for ble

BPV. Upon it ... do

V.

Voc. Not in B.P.V Vacancy
nor in any other old R.L 1st word in H.B list under T.
" " " Rep Comp " " "

I.P. 46 & Voc. BPV Valid } do
" " " Validity } valid'

I.P. 46 BP Vegetable veget'

" Voc " Vegetarian

Not in BPV Vegetarianism

in full Not in BPV Vegetate } ...
in full nor any other old R L " Vegetated } Pr & p. tense alike

Compare the whole class of Vegets.

2ᵈ p I.P. 46; Voc. B.P.V ... Version ... do

[a] Signifies that the dot must be inserted
2ᵈ p Voc. Not in BPV Conversion ... do

2ᵈ p " " Aversion ... do

Notes	Word	Abbreviation	
Not in B.P.V nor any other old R.L	Vexatious	vex'	
"	Vexatiously		
"	Vexatiousness		
Voc. "	Virtual		do
SP46; vir? Park. SP10 & BP Ver'	Virtue	Vert²	do
" Voc. do B.P.V. Ver'-Es	Virtuous	Vert²-Es	do
S.P. Not in BPV nor any other old R.I.	Virtuously		do
BPV	Void	Inserted for comparison	do
SP46 "	Of it		do
" Not in BPV.	Have had		do

W

Notes	Word	Abbreviation	
BPV	Warrant	warrant'	do
Not in BPV.	Warranted		
"	Warrantable		
"	We are in		do
"	Without own		do
Not in BPV nor any other old R.L	We are of, we are to have		do
"	Where of		do do
"	Aware of		do

BPV	We may be	do
Genl. B.P. do	We may not (p 168, R. 3)	do
Not in B.P.V. nor any other old R.L.	We meant (Inserted for comparison) "We meant, we meant to"	
	Were meant	wanting
"	We mention	
"	We were not	
Not in BPV	"Were it, where it"	do
	Were it not	do do
Voc; R.M; BPV	West Indies R.M	do
JP 46 Voc. BPV	Whatsoever	do
or BPV unlike	Whensoever alike	alike do
Not in B.P.V.	Where it	do
(Where it is not) BPV	Where its (or Where it is), dws,	do
Voc. BPV	Whereof	do
Not in BPV.	We are of, we are to have	do
	As are of	do
BPV	Which are	do
Not in B.P.V	Which were	do
BPV	Which are not	do
Not in B.P.V.	Which were not	do

Not in B.P.V nor any other old R.L	... ...	Which are of ...		do
"	...	Which were of	}	do
"	...	Which were to have	}	
"	...	Which are to have ...		do
"	...	Which were to have ...		do
{1 P 46 ... Park p 2" Not in BPV		Which had	...	do
Not in B.P.V	...	Which had not	...	do
" {Park 49	...	Which have	...	do
"		Which have had ...		do
1 SP 46 2d p { ' (joined) 9 Cr Not in BPV		Which it (See Wh. ought to h. had)	...	do
Not in B.P.V	...	Which ought	...	do
"	...	Which ought not	...	do
{B.P.V		Which w^d (or had) not	...	do
Not in B.P.V	...	Which ought to have	...	do
"		Which have	...	do
"		Which would have	...	do
"	...	Which ought to have had	...	do
"		Which have had	...	do
"		Which would have had	...	do
"		Which were	...	do
{ B.P.V		Which are	...	do

Notes		Word		
Not in B.P.V nor any other old K.		Which were not (See Which are not)		do
		Which were of (" " To have)		do
"		Which are of (or to have)		do
"		Which were have had, dws,		do
"		Which will it		do
Park which wd		Which would (or had)		do
Not in B.P.V		Which would have (See Which ought to have)		do
		Which would have had (See Which ought to have had)		do
		Which would not (or had not) (See Which ought not)		do
IP46	B.P.V. SK	While		do
"	" SK	Whi		do
Not in B.P.V		Wish it (SEE Shall it)		do
"		With our own		do
; BPV	Knot omitted	Working classes	K omitted	do
Not in BPV		Workman-men	n-hook for men	
IP46; Voc.	"	Worshiper		do
Not in BPV		Wretched-ly-ness		do

Y

Notes		Word		
heavy IP46 year-s	heavy B.P.V	Year-s-ly	light	See Yet in 2d list do
Yed heavy by instruction	"	You	light	See Beyond in 2d do

Part Second.

Present and Past Tenses.

§1. __Instruction and Practice Preceding the Hand-Book__. "The past tense of a verb that is expressed by a logogram, or by a contracted outline, may usually be written in the same way as the present tense; thus, the phonograph [Remember] may represent both Remember and Remembered, represent and represented. Subjected should be written or it may clash with Subject [ ]. The d may be added separately in any such case, for greater clearness." Par. 26, p. 18 of Isaac Pitman's Reporter's Companion. 4 ed. 1856.

(b). The preceding paragraph is as follows: "It will be found expedient to adhere somewhat closely to the rule for halving the letters, adding t only to the thin consonants when shortened, and d to the thick ones. Bright, plied, etc., should, therefore, be written thus; bright, plied. Exceptions are, of course, allowed in the past tense of verbs ending in t, as darted."

(c). All the old Phonographic instruction-books show that the general if not invariable practice, in both the corresponding and reporting style, was to write the past tenses in full except in case of word-signs or contractions which would not allow the regular formation of the past tense; thus, suspend, suspended, extend, extended, intend, intended, torment, tormented, intimate, intimated, regard, regarded, acquaint, acquainted

invite, invited, act, acted
accounted, occasion, occasioned (See
amply, complied, open, opened
consumed, abuse, abused, con
light, lighted, need, needed,
attend, attended, mend, men
want, wanted, suppress, suppre
exercised, possess, possessed
suaded, print, printed, plant,

§2. The Hand-Book Instruction and

(a) "Rem. 8. [p. 168]. It is usually allowable
for the reporter when a stroke or more can
to represent the past tense of a verb by th
ent tense; writing, for instance, Ses-Pe
of Ses-Pen-Ded [ ], for suspended; S
of Sten-Ded [ ], for extended; and
the context for the distinction between the
ciple may be employed in very many
senting the past tense of verbs not belon
of signwords; as in writing, Net-Me
Ent²-End, [=intend] for intended, Ter²-
for tormented, Ray²-Gerd, [=regard]
Kay²-Net [=acquaint] for acquainte
[=resort] for resorted."

(C) p.193, "Rem. 1. From the preceding list
excluded many contractions which m
in due time, be formed by the reporter
with the general principles of §237,
[☞] a large number of contraction
tenses or perfect participles, which
in accordance with the principles
above]

(d) From Part V, p 8., Rem. 1, near the c
reporting style, where the past tense o
ciple is expressed if more convenien
of the present tense, the laws of both an
are more fully complied with by writing En-Vert
Vershon. inversion, Con-vert convert-ed — Con

§2 continued (e) See numerous examples of this instruction in Part I of this Exhibit. See also the following mentioned examples from the "Specimens of the Reporting Style", pp. 31-2 of the Reading Exercises. lacerated, faded, accumulated, lifted, crowded, breathed their, prompted, who has accumulated

§3. Examples from the Reporter's Companion.

Note. The full form of the past tense is given in curves or indicated by dot lines.

Abstract-ed	Broken-hearted
Accomodate-d	Build-ed
Acquaint-ed BPV	Calculate-d
Admit-ted	Centre-d B.PV
Afford-ed	Challenge-d See Part I of this Exh.
Anchor-ed	Change-d "
Anticipate-d	The two preceding words fall under the old rule of word-signs and contractions, whose past tense can not be conveniently formed.
Ascend-ed	
Associate-d BPV	
Attempt-ed See under Tempt	Color-ed
Attract-ed	Concert-ed
Augment-ed	Conclude-d
Avert-ed	Constitute-d* See P.I of this Ex.
Await-ed	Contemplate-d
Bigot-ed	Contract-ed

* BPV

Convert-ed ( )
Cultivate-d ( )
Debilitate-d
Dedicate-d
Deduct-ed ( ) BPV
Deject-ed
Delight-ed (or)
Demand-ed ( )
Demonstrate-d
Denunciate-d
Depart-ed
Deprecate-d
Deride-d
Dread-ed ( )
Direct-ed ( )
Dislike-d ( )
Disappoint-ed ( ) BPV.
Distribute-d
Dispute-d
Divert-ed
Advert-ed

Doubt-ed ( ) BPV
Downhearted ( ) See Part I of Ex.
Downtrod-den ( ) "
Exaggerate-d
Exclude-d
Exhibit-ed
Expand-ed ( )
Extend-ed ( )
Extract-ed
Extricate-d
Forward-ed
Found-ed ( )
Forgot-ten (BPV)
Frustrate-d p. 29 R.C
Habit-ed
Hazard-ed ( ) See Part I of Ex
Hesitate-d ged ; H.B ; R.C. ( )
Husband-ed ( )
Illustrate-d
Immigrate-d

Inspect-ed
Insult-ed
Intend-ed
Interpret-ed (BPV)
Interrogate-d See Part I of Ex.
Intimate-d
Invent-ed
Invert-ed
Invite-d
Lament-ed See Part I of Ex.
Limit-ed
Merit-ed
Mitigate-d
Obstruct-ed
Operate-d (BPV)
Order-ed
Part-ed
Patent-ed
Penetrate-d
Persecute-d

Precipitate-d
Predestinate-d
Present-ed
Prevent-ed
Profit-ed (or)
Promulgate-d
Prosecute-d
Prospect-ed See Part I of Ex
Protect-ed
Public spirited
Recommend-ed (BPV)
Regard-ed
Regenerate-d
Regret-ted
Reiterate-d
Reject-ed
Remitted
Remonstrate-d
Render-ed (BPV)
Repeat-ed

Repent-ed

Report-ed

Repute-d

Respond-ed

Restrict-ed

Retort-ed

Retract-ed

Retreat-ed

Revert-ed

Revolt-ed

Reward-ed BPV

Round-ed

Rule-d

Soberminded

Speculate-d

Suggest-ed (word-sign) BPV

Superintend-ed

Support-ed

Surrender-ed BPV

Surround-ed BPV

Suspect-ed

Tempt-ed See Part I of Ex

Tolerate-d

Torment-ed

Transcend-ed

Uncontradicted

Underhanded

Unregenerate-d

Unsophisticate-d

Vegetate-d

Vindicate-d

Wait-ed

Await-ed

Warm-ed

Warrant-ed

Wound-ed BPV

Seventeen words only of this list occurred in the "Reminders" "Vocabulary" presented in the 2nd Book; hence the permutations given are here indicated by the [illegible] One of the seventeen words (Suggested) was provided with a word sign (logogram) and is an illustration of the rule [illegible] the past tense [illegible] the same as the present when the sign does not allow the regular formation of the past tense; the other words are written in full according to the old Phonographic instruction and practice

www.ingramcontent.com/pod-product-compliance
Lightning Source LLC
Chambersburg PA
CBHW030837300326
41935CB00037B/585

* 9 7 8 3 3 3 7 4 0 7 6 3 6 *